But I Still Love You

A Testimony of God's Unfailing Love

By Crystal A. Clemons

Edited by Johnny G.

Table of Contents

♡

Introduction

This book is dedicated to every single person on the planet that feels unloved, unworthy, disposable, or overlooked.

You are a beautiful treasure. God sees you. May this story bring you the hope and healing it has brought me.

All the glory to God.

A special thanks to my wonderful husband for patiently putting up with me forcing him to be my editor and helping me with this project. Also, to my kids who had to deal with a tired mom for over a week as I fervently, okay obsessively, worked on completing this book. Thank you to everyone in my life, who unbeknownst to them, has helped to love me back into a whole person. Every kind and genuine word of encouragement, act of love, or even a smile my way helps me to heal and see more of the good and beauty in this world. Thank you for being you!

Introduction

When I was a little girl, I thought I had a good idea of what love was. It was the Happily Ever After's of my favorite fairy tales and the whirlwind romances of the movies I watched where everything turned out alright in the end. It was when my Dad would scoop me up and plop me on his shoulders or tuck me into bed at night and make me laugh. Love was what I felt for my family and friends. It was something that was pure, unconditional, everlasting, saw the best in people, and was good. It was a protection from the bad in this world; a sanctuary. Love was never supposed to hurt… or so I thought.

My 'Love' story has been quite a journey through the many twists, turns, ugliness, and beauty. It has taken me through deep pits, dark valleys, and bouts in the wilderness. Through it all, I can see the love of God interwoven in the tapestry of my life. He is in every chapter, every line, even when I didn't realize it at the time. Though I am the author of this book, God is the author of my story. I present to you a glimpse of our Love Story.

PART ONE

Unhappily Ever After

One night when I was eight years old, I went to bed with a dad, mom, and brother. When I woke up the next morning, my dad and brother were gone. I was told for many weeks they were on a fishing trip. I wouldn't be told until much later the truth; that my dad had left with my brother to his new family and that my parents were getting a divorce. There was no fishing trip.

When you are a kid everything is new. You are constantly learning and assessing these new situations and experiences as good or bad, each one beginning to shape the foundation of your life. Until then, I felt I had a pretty normal life. I looked at the love between my parents and our little family of four as something solid and unchanging. I didn't realize love could change. I thought love was 'Happily Ever After' and enduring.

Shortly after my parent's divorce, my aunt and uncle got divorced. I had thought love was supposed to be permanent. Yet as I grew older I saw a shift where it became something fickle, conditional, and painful. Love became abusive, abandoned, and ugly, marred with the gashes of nasty words, cold shoulders, spitefulness, and indifference. "Love" became a curse.

It was six months after the separation until I finally got to see my Dad again, and even longer until I got to see my brother, though I had been able to talk to my Dad on the phone. My mom and I stayed at my grandparent's house for a while. Every time my Dad would call, they would talk so poorly about him, say bad things about him like how he had abandoned me and chosen a new family, how he wasn't taking care of me financially, etc. I saw and heard people I loved bad mouth another person I loved. A chasm began to separate sides of what was once a unity built on love.

Both my mother and father remarried within six weeks of the other in early '97 when I was nine. My Dad with his "mistress" and my Mom with a guy she had only known three months. I got to see my brother again. He came back to live with us but he was a different person, already getting in lots of trouble. I stayed with my mom and visited my Dad every other weekend and every other holiday. I didn't know where I fit in. My Dad had a new wife, a stepson, and a stepdaughter. I was told throughout the years by two family members how my Dad had a new family and he loved my stepsister more than me.

I was asked by my best friend's mom if I liked my stepdad. I remember hesitating, scared and unsure to tell the truth. I didn't want to be seen as a troublemaker or bratty kid. I choked out 'Yes.' I lied. It wasn't that I didn't like him, but I didn't like the way he made me feel. He made me feel icky, nervous, and bad in a way I couldn't consciously describe or even understand at the time. I didn't like how he made demeaning sexual jokes about my mom in front of his guy cop buddies and me. I didn't like how he swore, watched naked people and had naked "art' on our walls, undermined my mom, threatened and fought with my brother, yelled at our dog and was mean with her, and drank alcohol so much. I didn't like the way he acted… but I was only a kid and no one ever listened to me.

We got a new house, got settled as a family, and tried to work on our new normal. After about a year, my stepfather got more comfortable. My brother, seven years older than me and seventeen at the time, had already begun having major problems. We learned he had a drinking problem and had been doing drugs. A few years into the marriage, we learned my stepdad had a drinking problem too.

Many things happened, little and big, throughout the following years that began to unravel absolutely everything in my life. God, family, friends, love, stability. My household was in turmoil. At thirteen I was diagnosed with depression and medicated with Paxil. No one ever asked how my home life was. Not one. I was just told there was something wrong with me over and over again throughout the years. I was told I had a "chemical imbalance" and popping pills was supposed to cure my unhappiness. Meanwhile, the fights at my home got louder and more frequent. My stepdad yelled and cursed at my mom, calling her bad names, doors slamming at all times from early morning waking me up to late at night keeping me awake.

My brother spiraled downward too. Getting fired or quitting jobs, going from house to house like a train-wrecked gypsy, girlfriend to girlfriend, and winding up back with us for awhile. Every time he came back I got excited. My brother was one of my first idols, my heroes, and first loves. I loved my big brother and I always hoped when he came back he would rescue me. He saw enough in the house to see it wasn't right, but my brother was broken too and despite some of his better intentions, he couldn't save me because he first needed to save himself. My brother had been arrested, homeless, put in a mental health facility, and desperately wanted to get clean, all by the age of nineteen. My stepfather the cop encouraged my underage alcoholic brother to drink beer in the house because it was 'better" than drinking outside the home. He also continually throughout the years commented how he wished weed were legal and if he didn't get a headache from it he would smoke it. He would drink and drive. He hurt my mom, threatened my brother, and bad-mouthed every single member of my family, and every friend. Yet when he put on his uniform and badge he was a superhero to the community.

He was glorified over and over and over again by everyone but those who lived with him and actually knew the real him behind closed doors. I tried going to family members.

"Did he touch you inappropriately?"

"No."

Then it was shrugged off. I was told I just needed to grow up, that I needed to respect him for putting up and caring for me since I wasn't even his kid, how much he loved my mom to put up with me and my brother. All these safe adults we are told to go to when there was a problem just shrugged it off or told me I was bad for having a problem with the household. My mom would tell him everything I shared with her in confidence making it even worse for me in the house and among family members. No one listened. No one cared. I got blamed, so I stopped talking.

By my teenage years, my mom had sunk into a depression and spent many years sitting in a dark house on the couch watching television mindlessly, her mood shifting with the wind. I learned to adapt to her moods and run when she was in Mr. Hyde mode. I learned to do the same with my stepdad and my brother. Yet every time anyone else was around there were Kodak smiles and we were the "perfect family" … except for us troublemaker kids of course.

After realizing I had no one to go to and after so long of cramming it all inside, stuffing it down, it began to seep out and rise back up. At around fifteen I began cutting myself. It wasn't enough to die, barely even enough to bleed, but just enough to feel and release the pressure inside, like how some people smoke a cigarette. First, with a butter knife, then with scissors, until a full-on razor blade I picked apart from my disposable razors. I first had suicidal thoughts at thirteen that got worse and worse as the things within my household got worse and worse, yet no one ever asked about that. I was diagnosed with social anxiety disorder and given more pills then sent home to my nightmare. I couldn't handle the stress of school and bullies on top of everything else, so I was declared homebound and had a teacher come to the house once a week. Friends didn't understand. They, like everyone else, looked at the surface from the outside and saw parents who smiled, laughed, bought me things, and were funny. Their parents fought too. Their parents drank and were mean sometimes too. It was difficult to put into words exactly what it was, so hard to do when the scars were on the inside and not visible to the average person. So, yet again, the household problems were blown off and I became more and more isolated.

My Dad and his family moved out of state when I was in middle school, right before things started getting really bad. The distance separated us even more. Every time he didn't call on my birthday or Christmas, my mother continued to almost gloat about how horrible he was. My Dad wrote me beautiful things in my cards that helped me through the bad things being said about him and the lack of consistent communication, but over time the lack of communication made me begin to question around thirteen if he really had replaced me with his new family and if I was so easily discarded as being out of sight and out of mind. I had already had about five years of hearing the negative things from my mom and her family by then, so it all built up. *Was the awesome Dad who had been my first love and hero only a mirage? Was what my mom and her side of the family said about him and our relationship really true? Did he really love my stepsister more than me? Did he even really love me at all? After all, he wasn't there. My mom, stepdad, and her side of the family were…*

At fourteen, my maternal grandfather passed away. He had been a bright, shining light in my life. He always made me feel loved and was patient with me. He listened to me and seemed to value me, not like the others who treated me like just a kid. My grandpa treated me like a person with value. He loved me unconditionally, if not too much by spoiling me. He sacrificed for me. He was a treasure taken from me too soon and just before I really needed him the most.

~ THE BURNING BUSH ~

Then there was the whole *God Thing. Is God really real or just a fairy tale like Santa Claus? If God is real then what does that mean for my life? If God isn't real then is there something more to this life or is it all meaningless?* And about a billion and one other questions pertaining to life that permeated my thoughts as a teen.

When I was thirteen and just in my eighth-grade year at middle school, something happened to me that so shook me to the core I refused to utter a word to anyone about the incident until much later on in my life. A friend had invited me to her youth group one Wednesday night. I went to get out of my house. There they talked about stuff that went over my head and I started feeling scammed. I think she said there would be food, but it turned out to be like a recruitment process where they talked about God and asked us kids if we wanted to be saved. All of that stuff made me uncomfortable.

I became an atheist at eight years old after I was told that Santa Claus, the Easter Bunny, and the Tooth Fairy were all hoaxes and stupid games my family had been playing with me and lying to me about since I was a kid. When I asked two family members if God was real, neither answered me. That told me all I needed to know; that God was just a more important illusion/game to them than the others. So I became an eight-year old atheist despite being brought up in a "Christian" household. So church was just an escape to me.

The youth pastor did what I now know to be an alter call. During that whole time, something had been stirring in me, that despite all logic and reasoning, I felt such a strong urge to go up there even though I didn't even believe in God and certainly didn't want to participate in a delusion. God was for weak and silly people who needed something to believe in. I didn't need any of that, so I thought. My friend went up and I stayed behind. Meanwhile the urging grew stronger than ever, but struggling with severe social anxiety meant I rarely ever spoke and certain didn't do anything to draw attention, least of all go to the front where people would actually notice me. My legs were locked in place though my heart was moving towards the front.

All of a sudden, as my friend was in line waiting for the front to speak with the youth pastor and get prayer, me being alone in the seats with the few stragglers in other rows, something happened. All the noise stopped and got strangely quiet. The room began to expand as an insanely pure, bright, white light began to fill the room. I looked around frantically to see if anyone else was noticing this, but they were all oblivious. It was like I was watching them on a movie screen. Then this presence began to fill the front right-hand corner, just beyond the youth pastor. No one else noticed anything. It freaked me out royally and I was glued to my seat, panic rising. Without even believing in God, I understood that presence to be The God. I just knew. It was overwhelming realizing the real God I had thought was just a fairy tale was there, with me, in that room, and looking right at me. He made sure I knew it was me He was there for. He didn't speak, just let me accept what was going on. I couldn't stare straight at God, because I felt an overwhelming sense that this presence was greater than any royalty on earth and deserved even greater respect. Up until that point I hadn't even believed in God, yet there I was knowing in my blood that presence deserved the highest honors. I was terrified because my former concepts of God were either a Santa Claus in the sky or some great and powerful being watching us all with a trident waiting to strike us down and burn us into ash if we did anything wrong. I squirmed in my seat, then finally just sat there as I felt God's presence press a message into me. I looked His way and the feeling I got from Him was not of some angry dictator on a power-trip, but of love, warmth, and personality.

Though God deserved the highest level of respect, and I could feel His authority without it being spoken, He was coming specifically for me. He made sure I knew He was real and what He was really like. I felt a warmth and comfort from God that I had never before associated with my idea of God. God was peace, light, love, hope, warmth, comfort, and real. Once I understood that, I felt the presence was smiling at me, though I couldn't clearly see the face as the light was too bright. It was like looking at someone with the brightest sunlight right behind them, so the light masks much of the face. I was left not being afraid of God and having my concept of God forever changed. The noise started coming back until it was overwhelmingly loud with the chatter from a room-full of teens, the room went back to the normal size, and God's presence slowly left the room. I wanted to cry out to wait, to come back, but I felt the presence was just smiling at me, letting me know it would be ok. How I wish I would have kept that message with me throughout the years when I needed it the most.

As if that experience with God wasn't enough, my friend had come back to her seat. The service was almost over. That pressing to go up was still there and stronger than ever, but I figured my time to go up had passed as they were closing up service. All of a sudden, without me having said one word about the desire of my heart to go up to the front despite not understanding one jot of what it all meant, my friend grabbed my arm and pulled me to the front. She took me directly to the youth pastor still holding my arm and when it was our turn said, "This is my friend Crystal and she wants to be saved." BAM! I seriously had not spoken one single word to her about wanting to go up there, the least of all wanting to be saved, yet she drug me up there and I was nervous about what this "being saved" meant, my head was reeling from the events with God and then with my friend, yet my heart was content knowing in a way I couldn't consciously understand, that it was where I needed to be.

The youth pastor talked to me. It was all a blur. My friend was right there with me the entire time, like it was an unspoken mission. We never spoke of it, and haven't to this very day, and I never told her what had gone on. My brain couldn't even process enough to ask her why she did something so bold as to drag me up there without consulting me first and declaring I wanted to be saved when she had no conscious knowledge if I did or not. I pushed that experience deep within me because it was too huge for my teenage self to grasp. I was scared people would think I was crazy. I'd never heard any of my family talk about experiences with God like that, so I didn't want to seem any weirder. I was already learning I couldn't trust people, and God was just not the Pandora's Box of crazy I wanted to open in my life at that time. I thought about that experience many times throughout the years, and called myself a Christian because I thought all it consisted of was believing in God. I never cracked a Bible to read through or made any other effort to actually repent or follow Him. I just went with the motions like most everyone else around me.

~ FIRST LOVE ~

Shortly after my grandfather passed, a huge moment in my life occurred. After years of being the shy, overweight, geeky girl with glasses and braces who only dreamed of her Prince Charming, I had finally gotten my first boyfriend. I remember how shocked and excited I was. Someone finally really wanted to love *me*! He was tall, dark, and handsome too. Everything my naïve superficial fifteen-year-old self wanted in a guy *and* he was older. Two years older. Fifteen and seventeen are two different planets, especially between the genders both physically, emotionally, and developmentally. I was still fantasizing about boy bands and daydreaming of being a pop superstar and he was a strong, near-adult already physically a fully grown man who towered over me. Suddenly sex became a valid discussion, not merely something to giggle and fantasize about with my girlfriends. It was a very real thing suddenly and it scared the crud out of me, yet intrigued me at the same time. I knew I wasn't ready yet. I was still too young to deal with that. I'd always pictured the act of sex as a serious thing, meant to be preserved for my one true love, right after we got engaged and had that magical moment, and being married shortly after. It stirred up thoughts and feelings in me I wasn't prepared for.

I saw he loved me. He'd walk all the way across town just to see me and saved what little money he had to buy me a single rose ever so often. I had thought it was all I had ever wanted, but suddenly when it was right in front of my face I grew terrified. I started holding back, feeling angry and scared, and pushed him away. I saw things in him that concerned me, so I justified my fear by pushing him away even more. All I had witnessed was "love" being something so destructive and ugly. It destroyed, crushed, tore down, abandoned, abused, and hurt. Love was pain, and I was so afraid of being hurt even more. We broke up within a year and I developed a subconscious pattern of breaking up with boyfriends around six weeks. It was just enough time to enjoy the novelty and get close, but I pulled away before getting too close. It was the same with jobs, college classes, anything and everything I pulled away from when it started getting too close. Anytime anything potentially good was happening in my life, I got afraid and began to retreat into the safety of my turtle shell where at least no one new could hurt me. By then the thoughts permeated my head and heart into a deep-rooted belief that I wasn't deserving of love or anything good. The negative words my family had spoken over me my whole life became my truth. I was bad, ungrateful, manipulative, unworthy, disrespectful, fat, ugly, weird, a freak, picked last, easily replaced, untrustworthy, lazy, selfish, spoiled, a troublemaker, hateful, unlovable, in the way, no value, would never be successful, wrong, a drama queen, too sensitive, and more. I was also told by a close family member when I was seventeen that he wished I'd never been born. My own family members used me, manipulated me, and played deep mind games with me throughout my life. They spread lies about me to make themselves look better and cover their own inner ugliness. They convinced people I was those nasty things to isolate me further and keep me dependent on them. It made them feel good to be needed even if they didn't really like me. It's called Narcissism. I didn't know there was a word for it at the time. I began to believe what they said about me and how they made me feel. I felt worthless, like I had no value, nothing to offer the world, and that everyone would be better off and happier if I were dead.

I felt like a piece of trash and began to act accordingly. Trash doesn't have value…and neither did I.

PART TWO

But I Still Love You

By the age of nineteen I had spiraled so far downward I couldn't even recognize myself. I hated the girl I had been for she was the one not good enough to even be loved and treated well by the people who should have loved her the most. I consciously chose to distance myself from the shy, broken girl and tried so hard to be tough, strong in all ways, and the complete opposite of who I was. It worked, but not in a good way. In this effort to be this totally different person, I shattered my reputation and became even more of a joke which only dug me deeper into the pit. I did things I never thought I would or even wanted to, but I went along with this new image. Maybe this new girl wouldn't get hurt. WRONG! Except this time, she was hurting herself and others too. Inside I was dying even quicker compounded with the guilt, shame, and regret from my new lifestyle choices.

From the girl who had made straight A's, was in the gifted program and on Honor Roll at school, was always gentle, peaceful, and loving, encouraging, always smiling, hopeful and happy with a head full of dreams and a heart full of love to a snarky, dark, sarcastic, depressed, pessimistic, suicidal teen flunking out of classes with no hope for love or happiness, seeing no good in the world and daydreaming of death. Yet no one ever questioned about the home life. Not one.

By then I had been diagnosed as depressed, having social anxiety disorder, generalized anxiety disorder, bipolar, suicidal, and even homicidal. That last one was thanks to my mother being overdramatic. In my awkward teen years where I had difficulty communicating well, I blurted out in the middle of a bad time with my stepfather that I wanted to kill him. Teen Speak meant that I wished he would stop hurting my family and I so hated what he was doing. My mother took that as a literal threat, told that to the doctors so it got written down in my record, and shared with many other family members, giving them even more reason to look down on me and distance themselves from me. I was prescribed an anti-depressant, anti-psychotic, anti-anxiety, a sleeping pill, and an anti-nausea pill to combat the side effects of the other meds. Five prescription pills a day for a nineteen-year-old. They caused me to gain weight, have chronic fatigue, and my brain was in such a thick fog that I couldn't even remember conversations I'd had.

The solution to these diagnoses was to drug me up so I was even more of a shell of myself. It numbed me, like the walking dead, but it did absolutely nothing to cure me. The pain only increased and so did the symptoms. Nothing ever made it better because they never asked "Why?" The doctors just looked at me indifferently and scribbled a prescription on their notepad then collected their paychecks.

I choked back disbelief every time my parents sat in front of my doctor asking why and saying that all they wanted to do was help me. I would think of the countless times I had gone to each of them, separately then together in a family meeting, for the past six years, and each and every time they turned it around and blamed me then treated me poorly for daring to say they had problems that were hurting the family and causing my own problems. My brother had even gone to them as well. It made it even harder having to sit through and watch the show for the doctors. I wanted to scream at them, yell, throw something to get them to stop their lies. They knew full well what caused my problems. The anger raged and boiled within me, yet I had to keep stuffing it down because all of my outbursts only proved to everyone else that I was crazy, no-good, a troublemaker, and whatever other adjective they chose to describe me as.

No one saw me. No one got it. No one really helped. They just turned up their noses, looked down at me, and distanced themselves from me even more. They said I needed Jesus, but never once showed me the love and compassion of Him, just coldness and criticism. The louder I screamed, the more they hated me or distanced themselves from me in their own ways. I was supposed to just keep quiet, glue on my fake smile, and pretend. I had to be who they wanted me to be. I had done that for so many years, but I no longer had the strength to keep on with the charade.

Shortly after my nineteenth birthday I gave myself a present by checking myself into a behavioral health facility an hour and a half away. I hoped it would fix me. I spent three days there and it didn't do one bit of good to fix the problems except give me writing material and add a layer of depth to my story. However, at least there the doctors were nice and treated me as something close to human. I was able to talk with the other "guests" and even laugh and have a little fun. A golden moment for me was winning a game against the group with my teammate. Finally, I did something right and it took me being in a mental health facility to get the support and encouragement I needed to feel remotely human. Unfortunately, I was checked out and hauled right back into the problem. I had been forced to move back in with my mother and stepfather because at that point I was too damaged to function. I couldn't work. I could barely survive and was so immersed in pain that as my peers were starting college and planning for their futures, I was planning to kill myself. It consumed me.

After my voluntary visit, I fervently typed my journal entries into my computer in an effort to share at least some of my story. My only goal at that time apart from killing myself was to not let my pain die in vain. I wanted desperately to turn my negative into someone else's positive. I hoped that at least one person in the world would know they were not alone with the feelings they had and weren't the only ones going through what I was. Had I had someone like that, things might have been different for me. In my death, I prayed someone else would find some hope. I finished it in December. My brother was back living with us too. He was twenty-six then and just as much a mess as I was, just different symptoms. Mine was disorders, panic attacks, and agoraphobia. His was drugs and alcohol. We played Mortal Kombat in my room while we were both in a state of brokenness, both being in a form of suicide, yet wanting to help the other and for each other to be saved. Playing video games with my brother was probably the best memories I have of that time.

~ Christmas 2006 ~

We went to my aunt and uncle's house for Christmas Eve dinner. We dressed up and pretended we were a normal, healthy, happy family. It was expected of us. Smile through the backstabbing and put downs. Ignore the ridicule. Pretend everything is okay and happy is more than an illusion. Play the game. Pretend this is love and what they say and do doesn't hurt, because if you let on that it does, they will make an even bigger deal and taunt you even more. Suck it up and play along. Gift-opening. Food. Pretend smiles.

My brother and I left early with the baby his ex told him was his, but turned out not to be. He stopped by a gas station on the way home and got liquor. He drank when he got back and was already drunk and ready to go to sleep before long. He wanted to sleep except the baby was still awake. My brother was about to drug the baby with Nyquil to get him to sleep so my brother could sleep off the effects of his liquor. I intervened and wore the baby out naturally by playing with him, letting him crawl around on the floor, and tickling him while my brother had already passed out in his room. I took care of the baby and got him to sleep on my own, without any drugs pumped into his little body. I felt like it was a victory for the night. Then my mother and stepfather returned home. The baby was safe and my responsibility relieved for the night. The whole incident bothered me so much, my brother almost drugging that little baby, his own continuing alcoholism and spiral downward, the family strife, especially when it was Christmas Eve and supposed to be such a warm time. All it did was make the contrast even wider that we were not a healthy family and I was so tired of pretending, of having to pretend. I was tired of it all. It was always a fight. Always walking on eggshells for the next bomb to drop and family member to have an episode or fight. I was done living like that, but nothing else I had tried helped. I was so tired of fighting. I was mentally, emotionally, and physically exhausted. I couldn't take it anymore.

Meanwhile, I had been plotting my suicide. The pain was so bad that night. I waited until my parents had gone to bed and had been there for over an hour. The entire house was still except for me. I always stayed up late anyway. My silent strategy was always to stay up as late as possible while they were sleeping and everything was safe in the house, then go to sleep as soon as they woke up in the mornings so I could avoid them and their issues. If I stayed out of their way and tried as hard as I could to be invisible, things were mostly okay. I lived like that for a long time. While I waited to make sure they were all asleep I started taking my prescription meds. I took my daily dose, then more and more, particularly of the anti-anxiety and sleeping pill. I took a whole lot of Ibuprofen. I didn't want to feel death. My plan was to drink all the liquor in the household, which my stepdad kept in full supply, take every last one of my prescription pills, then slit my wrists one final time and be done with life and all the junk that came with it once and for all. It was going to be my Christmas gift to myself, to end my pathetic life in a miserable, ugly world full of darkness and pain.

I sliced up my wrists some, enough to draw a decent amount of blood, but not enough to cut the big vein and bleed out. My death was a process. I listened quietly to ensure they were all asleep. Just as I was about to get up to leave my room and drink all the liquor, I felt a sudden wave of cloudiness and fatigue hit me. I was so tired. I had deliberately not taken too many of my sleeping pills because I was saving those for right before the last cut so I wouldn't fall asleep before I finished. I didn't understand the sudden wave of exhaustion. I didn't have the energy to make it out of the room. I told myself I would just rest a little then finish the plan a little later. I still had plenty of time before morning when the household would wake up and I was likely to be caught and stopped. So I laid down on my bed just to rest for a little. I wound up passing out. How I know this is because the next thing I know I woke up to complete darkness.

I felt like I was floating in a long, dark tunnel or in outer space. I could feel absolutely nothing. I heard and saw nothing. My body felt completely light. I had no control over my body and could not move. I remember consciously trying to move parts of my body, but I couldn't. As my mind awakened more I remembered what I had been in the process of doing and wondered if I had already been successful and the pills had already killed me. I wondered if I was in the process of death or already dead and moving on to whatever new thing awaited me in another form of life. It was in that moment that I realized I didn't really want to die. I felt myself drifting towards this total darkness, like a black hole that I felt would be death, and I started trying to fight against it, but was still unable to move my body. I remember screaming out NO in my head and that I didn't really want to die. I screamed out in my head to "please stop this!" I slowly started to see more light and realized I was lying in my own bed.

I came more and more to consciousness to where I was fully awake, but my body was not. I literally could not move any part of my body. I couldn't turn my head, raise an arm, or even wiggle a toe. It was like my brain was cut off from the rest of my body and it royally freaked me out. If I had succeeded in suicide, I wasn't supposed to be awake for any of it. I was terrified I had woke up right in the middle of my body shutting down and I would be forced to be fully conscious as I slowly died. I was afraid of more pain and afraid of the act of death. I tried to assess the situation and see what state I was in with my limited mobility. I tried to lift a hand to check my pulse, but couldn't. I stopped trying to move and instead focused on my heart beating. I counted that I had three to four long, slow breaths in-between each heartbeat. I kept check of my heart beats for about a minute and it didn't increase. I realized that was dangerously low. It was then that I began to cry without tears, panic, and plead in my head. I started crying out to a God I wasn't even fully sure anymore that existed. The realization hit me so suddenly. *"Please. Please God. Please stop this. I don't really want to die, I just want the pain to stop. Please save me! I don't want to die. I don't. I made a mistake. Please stop this! I don't want to die, but I can't keep living like this anymore. Please, if you save me, then please make the pain stop. Please don't let me be hurt anymore. I can't take this pain anymore. I don't really want to die, but I don't know what else to do. Please get me out of this!"*

I very slowly regained control over my body. It was still difficult to move and only a little at a time. My heartbeat was still very slow. I was first able to turn my head. I saw the light on the wall. I turned it the other way and saw the light was from my television. The movie I had been watching was still on. I watched more of it as I waited to regain control over the rest of my body. Slowly an arm, then I could move my toes, until I was finally able to sit up and move from my bed to my computer chair where I immediately logged into the suicide forum I had been going to for help and someone else to talk to during the late night suicidal episodes. I stayed on the computer until the early morning hours when dawn was close to breaking to ensure I would get through the night, then I went to sleep with the realization that I had to at least try to live one more time.

The fact that suicide wasn't really what I wanted stunned me, then I remembered my dream of how I had longed to go study art in Paris and sip coffee and write at an outside café with the Eiffel Tower within view. I remembered how I wanted to study abroad for the bulk of my twenties, being safely away from everyone and everything I had ever known. I held to that dream and tried to give another shot at life. I prayed to God that I would give him a year and a half, until my twenty-first birthday, to stop the pain and give me something worth living for. The strongest desire of my heart was for Him to give me just one reason to live. I prayed it and made an agreement that if He showed me that one reason to live by the time I turned twenty-one then I would never think of suicide again and I would dedicate the rest of my life to living. If He did not and my life and situation didn't get better, then I would have a final celebration with my closest friends, say all my goodbyes, then once everyone had left I would kill myself alone in my room on my twenty-first birthday and be done with it all. A year and a half was a long enough time for God to work, so I figured.

After the Christmas Attempt, I shared parts about my attempt with my family. I showed my mom my scars in the morning on Christmas day as I rolled up my black sleeves and just stared, lying in bed, no energy or desire to move. I watched her cry. I wondered if she realized she had a part in the scars. I wondered how she could claim to love me when she was the one who had ignored all my attempts to talk and warn her before it got to that point. I wondered when she would finally get it and step up to save me like I kept expecting her too, to put her foot down, to protect me… but she never did. She just kept asking "why?" when she knew the answer all along. I had told her repeatedly in various ways for six years.

More doctor's visits, more pills, then I got a place of my own. I couldn't stay in that household environment any longer. I used every bit of savings and some help from my parents. My stepfather supported me financially only to get me out of his house, so he told another family member, and I was perfectly okay with it. Getting away from the toxic environment was a good thing, but being alone to deal with the wave that came with it was not. I quickly found a new plague of trouble. Being alone meant dealing with the suicidal urges alone and the darkness coming on in waves stronger than ever. I felt haunted by dark figures at night that would taunt me and everything got worse. I was scared in my own home. During the day was okay, but the night was when it got really bad.

To stave off suicide I grabbed anything and anyone coming my way as an effort to save myself for one more day. My goal was just one more day, one more day. I couldn't think ahead to even a week at a time as I was struggling so hard to just get through one more day. I had a random guy I met on the internet that I'd been talking to stay with me for a few weeks. He introduced me to smoking pot and the term 'wake-and-bake.' I'd never wanted to do drugs before and always despised the very thought of it, having been a proud member do the D.A.R.E. program, but at that point I clung to it like a life raft. I had to see if it could save me. It didn't. Prescription meds didn't work so weed and alcohol became my next experiment. I had parties on weekends just to keep people around me because I wasn't suicidal when people were around, only when I was alone. I went through months of parties where I'd always get drunk to try to numb the pain and that beast within, adding countless one-night stands and drunken hook-ups to the mix with people who didn't love me at all. It further added to me feeling like I was worthless and of no value. I felt even more disposable, yet this time more and more shame and regret added to my already hurting heart. I was embarrassing myself, but had begun to spiral so far out of control that I could no longer stop it. It was a vicious cycle.

One guy I dated during that time was eighteen years older than me. I was nineteen. I don't need to say what the basis of our relationship was or what I meant to him, but at least he bought me food and a few things, he took me out to movies, and I was able to have a little fun with him. When I was with him I was alive. That mattered more to me than anything else at that time. Further and further I sunk, along with my once clean reputation, further perpetuating the belief I was a failure as a human being and better off dead. Nothing fixed the problems. No one showed up on a white horse to save me. After the parties were over and people went back to their own lives, the problems remained and the haunting of my suicide would come back with a vengeance. I tried countless self-help books, drugs, sex, alcohol, rock and roll, and meditation. Not one single thing helped.

I was Baker Acted (involuntarily admitted to a mental health facility) once in March of 2007 and again in April. The last time in April was the worst. I ran from my counselor's office and hid. The cops found me and I resisted. They pounded my head into the ground, tore my sweater, and left me with a black eye. They had guns and other weapons and cornered me when I was all by myself. I was used to cops being jerks and getting away with it because of their shiny badges and uniforms that made them invincible, even being labeled as "heroes" of the community. I was handcuffed, taken to the hospital to get checked out, and had to wear a neck brace. I had bleached my hair as the first step in the process of dying it pink. Bleached hair and near-albino pigmentation does not a pretty picture make. I lay in that bed reeling from the events of the day wondering how I had gotten there. To make things worse, my mother who had been with me at the counselor's office when I was Baker Acted called all the family to tell them what had happened. My aunt and uncle paraded around my hospital bed and just stared at me like I was a freak. I felt just like a monkey in a cage meant to entertain and disgust the onlookers. Knowing my mother did what she was so good at and turn everything into something about her, a typical narcissist trait, there was no telling how many people had heard about my ordeal by then. It was already humiliating without having everyone else in the family know, but my privacy was never a concern to anyone. I felt even more isolated, alone, misunderstood, and worse because this time was public humiliation added to the list. I had no one. Not really. I was alone in my battles. Nothing could save me. I quietly began plotting my suicide yet again in my head. I would wait until I got to my room in the mental health facility to do it. I would either quickly punch the mirror in my bathroom, shatter the glass, and shove it into the major artery in my neck, or quietly while I was in bed pretending to sleep (a skill I had mastered over the years) I would patiently and strategically wrap my bed sheet around my neck and strangle myself all while my one-on-one nurse sat in her chair unaware. I had a solid plan and a back-up plan. Failure was not an option. I knew it'd be worse if I attempted with witnesses and failed. I'd be seen and treated as even less than human than they already treated me. They all already looked at me and didn't see me, just like my family, just like they do homeless people on the street.

I felt secure and happy with my plan. I felt fully content and at peace with it. There was no turning back from public humiliation. I hadn't had anyone before and I really wouldn't have anyone after I got out. What was the point in trying anymore?! I had absolutely nothing left to fight for, but then something happened.

As I was left alone in that room on the hospital bed waiting for results to see if the fight with the cops left me more injured than just the visible black eye and scratches, feeling lower than dirt, so alone and so unloved, the room began to expand. The yellowish hospital light turned an amazing bright white. Within that light came a strong presence from above, one I knew to be God because it was the same experience of the room expanding and super bright light with the same familiar presence as I had experienced in my first "Burning Bush" moment when I was thirteen. Just like before, everything went completely quiet and God's presence filled the room. I was nervous, same as before, and uncomfortable. This great big presence was near me, there just for me, with a message for me, just like before. Slowly His presence filled the room as I grasped what was happening. Similar to what one would feel if Royalty or a favorite celebrity entered the room, was a similar reaction to how I felt being before this Great Presence. I knew it was bigger than me and somehow without being able to understand I just *knew* this presence was God, *the* God, again. He took me outside myself. His presence was above me and He showed me His view of me from a downward angle. Small, frightened like a wild animal, with bleached hair, a neck brace, and a black eye. I didn't look like myself at all on the outside. It was not a pleasant sight and I squirmed and tried to look away.

"Look at you," He said.

He showed me that same angle of me in the hospital bed at present, then, *"Look* at you!" and an ugly and painful montage of the dark lifestyle I had embraced. The partying, string of hook-ups, drinking, damaging my body, profanity, and deep sin I was immersed in… all of it shown to me like a movie. I tried to shut it out and look away again, but God firmly made me face it all. I forced myself to look after His words. I did. I watched. It was so hard, so ugly, and so not the real me. That was not how I was supposed to turn out. Then His voice came again, less forceful and more gentle with a sadness to it, "Look how far you've strayed." It was brutal having to face it all. He showed me even more. The stuff I tried to bury within me, the things I'd done in secret, yet it clearly wasn't a secret to Him. I felt disgusted with myself for how far I'd gone down that road and even lower and more deserving of suicide as a punishment. I felt of even lesser value and more humiliated seeing all of my shame and the ugliness played out like a film strip in a vision. His voice interrupted my thoughts of deep shame with the most profound statement I'd ever heard, *"…but I still love you."*

Those words baffled me. It was tender. Like what my own earthly father would say and how he would say it, with deep pain seeing me act in ways that weren't me and that were hurting me. I could never accept that anyone loved me. My own family didn't really, yet God Almighty, Creator of the Universe, most powerful being in the world, who saw every single one of my mistakes, said He still loved me. The real kind of love. The deep one that was strong and powerful. The true love kind of thing, like no one had really shown me in a very long time. All my sins should have repelled Him from me and warranted me being cut off and quickly cast into Hell for a deserving lifetime of more pain and torture, worse than I'd been experiencing on earth. Yet in spite of all my sins, He claimed to still love me. Nothing else could have shocked me more.

The message continued, *"Now, leave the path you are on and come to me."* He gave me another clear vision, but this time of a dirt road. On one end was where I was currently. It was filled with darkness, all types of sins, ugliness, and corruption. There He was not. There held my suicide and I clearly saw that road end in my destruction, either by my own hand or others dragging me down into it and laughing mindlessly along the way. It was filled with darkness, fire, depression, and more pain and torture. It was filled with illusions that were artificial and only pulled me closer to destruction. The middle of the road was empty and on the opposite end of the road was God and all of Heaven behind Him, full of the bright pure white light. He was waiting for me, with arms outstretched and smiling, waiting for me to get there so He could embrace me and take me in. The vision showed my ways of my destruction on the path where I currently was, all the ways it could end horribly and unfulfilling for me, then me turning from it and walking toward God. The closer I moved toward God in the vision, the freer and lighter I got. The heaviness and darkness left me and I began to smile with each step until once I was closest to Him was when I finally felt fully happy and at peace with no darkness at all in or around me. I was shown that the way where I was in darkness was full of people, but the way to Him I would be walking all alone with only Him to keep encouraging me on. God's presence stayed with me for a while longer until I abandoned my plan of suicide for a choice that would change my life in ways I never could have thought of at the time. I consciously chose to be that girl in the vision that left behind the darkness and started walking toward God. I had it deeply pressed into me that it was the only way I would ever truly be free of the pain and suffering, the only way I would ever experience true Goodness and be the real me. God showed me that all that awaited me after death, at that time, was more pain, torture, and darkness, but worse than I'd ever experienced before or could imagine. God's presence left once I had fully received and cognitively understood the message. The size of the room went back to normal, the bright light faded, and the noises came back. I hadn't realized before then how small, dark, and loud that room was. Then I was left to process the second encounter I'd had with God in my life. It forever changed me. That was the day I first decided to follow God.

My suicide plan was thwarted by God so I was stuck dealing with the aftermath of my second Baker Act in two months and the public humiliation. I didn't see how things could get much worse for me. I felt at rock bottom and only a miracle could pull me out of the mess. Since suicide was no longer an option thanks to the God Experience, the only way out was through.

The not very nice or helpful doctor wanted me to give him a plan. I learned that in the mental health world they really liked plans, particularly ones that didn't include killing yourself and were as close to their definition of "normal" as possible. I was treated like a criminal rather than a victim and someone who needed help simply because I was hurting and too broken to function "normally." I scrambled to come up with a plan in that room looking across at a doctor that I knew didn't give one real flip about me and got so angry right then and there that I determined if I got out of that mess alive I would become a psychologist to combat his insensitivity and lack of actual care. People like me needed love and genuine care, not more rude, uncaring people in the world that only saw a problem and not a person. I could go back home to get that.

The only semi-feasible and coherent plan I could concoct that wasn't snarky (because those dudes didn't like snarky) and might aid in my getting stamped and released was an idea that pressed into my head and clicked in my heart. I would go to my Dad's when I got out. The not nice doctor seemed to like that plan and I breathed an inward sigh of relief. However, going to my Dad's seemed about as far a stretch for me as it was to be normal. He lived in another state and our relationship had been strained over the years for various reasons. I still loved my Dad deeply, but I was wounded that he wasn't there for me and worried what my mom said was true and he didn't really love me at all. I was worried if I did go that I'd be in the way and no one would want me or that his new family would resent my presence. I was scared of it being like how it was with my mom and stepdad. I would have rather held onto the good memories I had with him than risk that relationship being shattered too. However, I kept feeling a peace and a pressing to go. I so wanted to be with my Dad, but I was so scared of the unknown. Thankfully, my mother was super helpful at giving me the courage to go because she was so unpleasant once I got released. It was like full-on Mr. Hyde on steroids mode with her digs and personal attacks. I knew I had to go before I punched her in the face or told her exactly what I had been stuffing down since my Dad left her, and that it would have made everything even worse for myself. I couldn't get away from her fast enough. During that time God was pressing into me in another vision and message that I would go up to my Dad's and meet the man I would spend the rest of my life with. That was an exciting thought and certainly the most promising prospect I had at the time. Stay and continue to get treated like a subhuman, or take a leap and find my One. Hmmm…

Shortly after that I packed my little car with as much of my belongings as possible and flew on the road to my new adventure. My Dad had agreed to let me stay with him on the conditions I went to church and A.A. meetings. I agreed. I would have agreed to just about anything in order to get away from my mother and stepfather and to spend some time with him. A.A. meetings I was cool with. Church, however, was something I had loathed for a very long time and was so not looking forward to scary people with screw-on smiles and big hair who clapped a lot with a Southern twang and told me all the ways I was wrong. I was scared of and repulsed by church, but figured I'd cross that dreaded bridge when I came to it. As someone who had never had healthy boundaries before and was also used to being controlled and manipulated, I chafed and bucked inside at my Dad's conditions. The funny thing was that even with that rebellion inside of me, I understood that my Dad's conditions weren't meant to manipulate or control, but to help me in the ways he best thought he could. They weren't vindictive, asinine, or self-serving, they were logical, healthy, and actually loving. I respected him more for trying to place healthy boundaries in my life, something that was foreign to me since he had divorced my mom. My Dad gave me those conditions because he loved me, and that made me love him even more. I took a huge leap leaving behind everything I'd ever known to the unknown that awaited me. For an agoraphobic who needed security and some form of stability and an escape to prevent a panic attack, every single bit of that journey was huge for me. I had lived the bulk of my life up until then locked in my bedroom for days and weeks on end to prevent a panic attack from even seeing people in the household, or while driving, and I couldn't even talk on the phone without having to talk myself through a panic attack. It was horrible the state I was in and the leap was terrifying, but I knew what it would be like if I didn't do it. The unknown was the best option I had at the time, and I kept that promise from God in my head to keep me moving forward. Getting in my little car and driving away from all the problems was amazing and so liberating even if it was terrifying.

The first day at my Dad's I did indeed meet the man whom I would spend the rest of my life with. As soon as I saw him I had another clear message from God and He was telling me that young man was the one. I sure didn't expect God to work that fast. My heart leapt and excitement coursed through my veins until I found out he was married. Then I scratched my head and wondered if I really was crazy or God was wrong. I sure wasn't going to spend the rest of my life with a married man.

My Dad didn't replace me with his new family. He really did love me as I'd known in my heart all along. My stepfamily didn't reject me either. I got to talk with them a little more and began to question some of the things my mom had told me, but still stayed on alert, wondering if they really loved me or were just tolerating me and would turn out to backstab me like so many other family members had. Keeping people at a distance had become a specialty of mine. I so enjoyed and craved that time with my Dad and this new family I hadn't ever really gotten to know that much in ten years, yet I was still feeling out of place seeing that my Dad wasn't exactly the Dad I remembered from when I was a kid. He had this whole new life and I was learning so much about him that I'd never known before.

A few months later, the married guy that I'd thought was "him" wasn't exactly married anymore. A few months after that I found out that this guy was the father of the baby I was going to have and that the vision was true. I would be forever linked to this man. I thought marriage would come next. We had moved back down to Florida and were living together because I realized with my Dad that I couldn't get away from all the problems try as I might. My brother had been living with him too and I saw firsthand how bad and deep-in my brother had gotten. It depressed and distressed me so bad I had to flee back to the strange comfort of familiar territory where I'd spent nearly two decades of my life. I needed my friends. I needed familiar. It was shortly before my twentieth birthday that I took the pregnancy test that came back positive. I sat and stared in disbelief. I was terrified and excited at the same time. I hadn't really had much experience with kids up to that point, and even less with babies. I could barely even take care of myself at that point and I was still struggling to get a foundation beneath me and get out of the pit I was in. I expected marriage and domestic life to come next. The father and I had been having problems. He had been fine for the first bit when we moved, but once he got his job he changed and became distant, cold, demeaning, and sexually abusive. I found myself trapped again and completely over my head. I'd gone back to my mom hoping she'd help me by giving my advice. She was best when she was needed. Once I found out about the pregnancy I pushed thoughts of leaving him away and thought the baby that he had talked so much before about wanting would be what would fix him and get him back on track. I was so sick in the early stages that I wound up being hospitalized for dehydration. I couldn't keep anything down and couldn't stand without getting dizzy and weak. Being so sick, my focus was only on my health and the unborn child's. I didn't pay attention to anything else. If I had been more alert, I might have realized his sudden personality shift and all the weird things he had started doing during that time was because he had picked up his drug habit again.

In mid-October, about six weeks after finding out about the baby, he left with his dad and I never heard from him again. He left me with pocket change all alone with our unborn child. I was even more terrified. I'd been rejected and abandoned once again. Again, I was unlovable, but this time, my baby was abandoned and rejected too and that made me angry. Instead of marriage and getting my Happily Ever After with the man I would spend the rest of my life with, that man from the vision turned out to be my son. His biological father was only the channel to get to that "one man" God told me I would spend the rest of my life with. The waves of pain at being left and alone in that situation knocked me back down for a while.

I was broke, too sick to even think about working, and still struggling to get better mentally and emotionally. I had given up drugs before the pregnancy and alcohol as soon as I learned I was pregnant. That was easy. No way would I bring a child into that mess. Even though I had never wanted biological children, only wanting to adopt or foster kids, I still had a huge heart for protecting life; especially helpless, innocent babies. I couldn't register that I was a mother. It was so Twilight Zone for me and not at all fitting into my plan. The biological father of my child chose a lifestyle of drugs and irresponsibility over family. That wasn't part of the plan either. Being too sick to work, no money, pregnant and single meant I had no choice but to go back to the place I had started and had tried in vain to get away from. My mother and stepfather took me in.

Nothing had changed in their household. There was hardly enough food, but the liquor was always fully stocked. My plan had been to work hard and get a job throughout my pregnancy, saving up enough money to get a place of my own after the baby was born. However, I stayed too sick throughout the entire pregnancy to even seriously consider getting a job. I couldn't even walk a minute without getting weak and lightheaded and I didn't just have morning sickness, but all-day sickness. It was miserable. Meanwhile my mother was hunting down groups for families of alcoholics and not getting much luck. Finally, after ten years, she began to acknowledge that her husband had a drinking problem. She grabbed a pamphlet and ticked off many of the boxes that indicated signs of an alcoholic as well as what life was like for the families of. All I was thinking of was that I was bringing a child into all that mess. No job, no money, no stability, no support, no experience, bad environment, no clue how to raise a kid, and single. I was a prime candidate for abortion.

I had threatened the biological father with abortion if he left in hopes he'd realize it wasn't all about him anymore and his actions had very serious consequences. However, as soon as I said that ugly world I felt it choke in my mouth.

Then I got a vision of this little baby inside my womb like it was waving its' hands trying to get my attention saying, "Hey! Hey! I'm right here! Hey! Mom! I'm right here!" I saw a very real vision of this tiny and fragile life inside of me and knew in an instant abortion was something I could never go through. I was the kid that at age seven held a funeral for a grasshopper that I had vigilantly killed then felt such remorse I dug a grave for it and even marked its grave with a small cross I made out of twigs. No way could I have a hand in murdering my own child, this innocent little life that depended on me for protection. No matter how bad my situation was, I knew abortion was never an option, but adoption was.

I knew everything was stacked against me and it would take a miracle to survive it. I didn't want kids of my own anyway. My family looked even further down on me. My own grandmother couldn't find any positive things to say about me to her friend who had asked about me. Judgment, condemnation, criticism. Sting upon sting. "Family" pouring more salt onto an already bleeding wound. Suddenly it was my fault for being pregnant and single. It was my fault the father left me and chose drugs over me and the baby. It was my fault I was pregnant. It was my fault I was too sick to work. It was my fault the only choice I had was to move back in with my parents. Not in college, no job, no hope, single unwed mother, no good, a burden. That was the support I got during my pregnancy from "family." God was supposed to be showing me a better life, a pain-free life, but I was only getting hurt more and the situation even worse. It wasn't just me suffering anymore, but now there was this life inside of me that was being brought into that mess too. Something had gone terribly wrong and I had no clue what to do. There had been somewhat of a freedom before. If things got bad in the house I could take off in my car and run away to wherever it was safe. I could be homeless and live in my car and it wouldn't matter. I couldn't do that with a baby. Having a child meant I was responsible for a life other than my own. I couldn't just up and leave, I had to stay and fight. I had to fight to give the child a solid foundation and stability. Kids needed and deserved that, yet it was something I couldn't even provide for myself at the time.

I spent the duration of my pregnancy while I was too sick and stuck in bed, pondering my life and that of my unborn child. The question being how it was all going to work. Instead of panicking, which I had every logical reason too, I strangely felt a sense of calm and peace throughout it all. I so strongly felt I was wrapped in God's protection that I never feared after that. Rather than just jumping impulsively and then failing as I had so many times before, I embraced the clarity I felt from being off the prescription drugs and for the first time really began to think through my life, weighing every single thing in a calm, rational manner. I did my best to try to form a plan that would secure a foundation for that of myself and my unborn child. I wasn't sure at that point if I would give my baby up for adoption or not. I felt the peace of God wrap around me strongly for the first time in my life. I felt like God had me and the baby wrapped in His arms and I could not explain why I had such a peace in spite of the turmoil. I prayed for God to lead me, before I really knew how to pray. Lying in my bed one day I felt clarity, peace, and excitement about going to college to get a degree in Psychology. Rock star and actress were given up since agoraphobia didn't mix too well with those careers and they were too fickle of jobs to be a responsible choice for a baby of a single mom. Instead, I realized that all throughout my years, people seemed to naturally be drawn to me for guidance and wisdom, despite my own lack of it in my own life. Plus, I loved the feeling of helping people through their problems and being there for them. It gave me a small sense of purpose when I could help others. Besides, the world was plenty broken and ugly. A degree in Psychology with aspirations of my own practice gave me job security. I had a plan; a real, solid plan.

Then I envisioned the practical side of doctor's visits and friends for my child. Talking on the phone already sent me trembling and I had to exert so much energy beforehand to just get through it without panicking. How could I survive those doctor's visits and meeting new people to ensure my child had friends? I knew then that I absolutely refused for my child to suffer through my own messes. My problems were my own, not my child's. I refused then and there to let my own setbacks set my child back. Whatever it took, no matter how hard it was, I determined to fix myself so I didn't break my child. My personal vow to that unborn child was to never let the child be hurt the way I was. I was going to ensure that child had a better life, even if it meant I wouldn't raise the child as my own, but would pass the torch on to someone else who could.

Because of my unborn child, I began to work on myself. Baby steps. Bill Murray's face kept popping up in my head from the movie 'What about Bob?' Baby steps to talk on the phone. Baby steps to go to the grocery store. Baby steps to smile at the stranger. Baby steps to the doctor. That was how I pep talked my way through my early and mid-twenties when panic attacks still threatened me in public settings, driving, and talking on the phone. Slowly, one baby step at a time, I got to be able to go to the store without a panic attack and it eventually progressed from there to where I could be semi-normal and functional. My desire for my child to be unharmed motivated me every day of my life to get better, to *be* better.

My baby was born fully healthy. He was beautiful in a crinkly red smooshy baby kind of way. I was also freaked out because I didn't know babies looked so weird when they were born. I'd only ever seen movie babies. He had ten fingers, ten toes, and healthy lungs. He was a perfect weight and length. Not deformed. Not a freak with a cyclops eye or arm sticking out of his head that I thought the spawn of someone as messed up as me would have. No, he was totally perfect and I was in awe.

Sparing details, I had a traumatic delivery to where I wound up losing over 5 ounces of blood and became anemic from it. I immediately had to be stitched up, but after two hours and excruciating pain, the midwife put me into surgery with glorious anesthesia. When I was being wheeled off and separated from my newborn baby, this heaviness gripped my heart that almost broke it. Suddenly I was so afraid of dying. I was terrified that I had just gotten this miracle in my life, but like everything else, it would be yanked away before I could enjoy it. I had two close friends watching over my little guy that made me feel a little better. I knew my one friend was a natural mother and would always protect him. I silently prayed for God to not take me. I didn't die, but I did have difficulty waking up from being knocked out for surgery. I woke up just in time to hear the nurse telling another nurse to get me Demerol. By the goodness of God, I was able to force myself to speak out "I'm allergic" as I struggled to lift my arm with the red bracelet that clearly had the words Demerol allergy written on it. The anemia had me shaking so bad it knocked my knees together which made the pain from my stitches and reparative surgery even more excruciating. I felt like I was in a literal nightmare. I hadn't even gotten to really hold my baby yet. Nothing was how it was supposed to be.

My baby was born at 6:57 p.m. and it wasn't until after midnight that I was wheeled back from surgery and finally able to be with him. I was so upset that everyone else got to spend time with him before me, but those moments getting to really see him and hold him meant everything. That baby was inside of me. My body did that! That *whole* thing was inside of *me*! Two days later we got to leave the hospital and start our new lives together. The next few months, instead of getting to fully enjoy my child, I was in the stages of physical recovery with the pain so intense I was again very limited to what I could do. I needed help bathing, going to the bathroom, and everything with my baby. Bending down to pick him up or put him in his bassinet pulled at my stiches in places no stitches should ever be and sent me into tears each time. I hated that I couldn't get to bounce him or play with him. I could barely smile because I was in such a state of deep pain. It was survival mode for me and focusing on my recovery. Because of my extensive injury from childbirth, again, a job was not an option and I was left dependent on the very people I needed to break away from. It sent me scratching my head and questioning God's plan yet again. Maybe He hadn't heard me or I hadn't stated the agreement clearly. He was supposed to make my life better and get me out of the pain, but instead I was only being hurt more and more. My heart was broken from the father of my child leaving us, as well as the residual issues from adding the sexual and verbal abuse to it. I was a single mother with no money. Then I had a horrific birthing experience and in the worst pain I'd ever gone through in my life that lasted for months and I still have to deal with from time to time. How was any of that better?! God so had a very cruel sense of humor or a serious misunderstanding of the word 'better.'

About four and a half months later, I was recovered enough that I could slowly do things for myself and get back to whatever normal was. I had my closest friends over to watch my favorite movie, then we went out to dinner to celebrate my birthday. I ordered a hard strawberry lemonade and only drank half of it. It was the first time I legally could order one and the irony was that I didn't even want it. My child meant more to me than drinking. I so enjoyed the time with my girls, but I had my baby in my head the whole time and I just wanted to get back to him.

When the clock struck after midnight, I was back with my baby holding his precious body in my arms as I celebrated my twenty-first birthday. I had a smile on my face looking down into his. It was then that it hit me for the first time the significance of that moment. That was when I was supposed to kill myself. My whole plan had been to kill myself on my twenty-first birthday at exactly that time. Instead I was holding my baby and feeling the first bits of this unexplainable joy that I'd never before felt. For the first time in my life I had something real, something tangible and beautiful of my own. If it weren't for my son and my desire to protect him, I would have gone through with my plan of suicide. I looked down at that little bundle who already had a great personality and was even more in awe that this tiny thing had saved my life.

Then the tidal wave of realization hit me like a freight train at full speed; my tiny son was the answer to my prayers I had so desperately prayed a year and a half before. He was my one reason to live! That little life gave me back my life. He began to soften my hurting heart. He made me fight to better myself and chase after what was right and good. He made me get up every day and press on despite the obstacles and impossibilities in our lives, one baby step at a time. He made me feel love and taught me what true unconditional love was. He made me put down my walls and embrace life, love, and all the good that can come from it. He gave me hope and purpose with feelings of joy and delight. He opened my eyes and had me marveling at the beauty of my own body that could finally do something good all on its own. That little baby with the inquisitive eyes who always put his little hand on my face before he could fall asleep was what saved my life. Something so tiny was so powerful and was God's gift to me.

The only reason I kept fighting in the years to come through more heartbreak with a failed marriage, nasty and verbally abusive in-laws, poverty, hunger, and deeper and darker pits was my son. I couldn't abandon him because then he'd be an orphan. I couldn't entrust his care to just anyone. I was his protector and I couldn't fail him. The beauty was that God saved my life by literally giving me life. He knew the only thing that would save me and make me fight hard enough through the storms was by giving me a little life to protect all on my own. Had his father stayed, had my family been more supportive, had I felt I had anyone I could truly trust to raise him up in the way God told me he was supposed to be raised, I probably would have killed myself. By God placing those painful obstacles in my life, they were actually His blessings of protection. Every day I had a purpose. I had a reason to get out of bed despite the inner pain and fear of what our future would be. I had a small, precious, innocent life that depended solely on me. It was overwhelming, yet amazing. My son opened my heart and brought me back to life. He made me laugh. He put passion back into my soul and made me remember what it was like to be a child, and all my hopes and dreams that I had let wither away. I began to smile and truly mean it for the first time in my life. For the first time ever, my heart was truly happy even when everything around me stunk.

My focus was on my baby and caring for him instead of the mess around us. I would turn on music and dance with him in the kitchen when he was a baby and we had finally gotten a place of our own. His smiles and laughter were my heartbeats and warmth in a cold, cruel world. I read him stories and dared to dream with him during the day while at night I battled exhaustion desperately trying to find a good job where I wouldn't have to ditch him to some random babysitter and the fear of leaving him with a stranger, all while trying to pursue my Psychology degree and wondering how I would get enough money to pay our bills and enough energy to get me through each day. It was during those times with seemingly impossible mountains in my path that my relationship with God grew stronger.

God had taken the destructive path I was on and gave me the one thing and the unfavorable circumstances He knew would ultimately save me. It also meant I would never be alone again. My son would never leave me. We would be forever united by the beautiful bond between mother and son, and our unique circumstances.

I had a family of my own. I had a true love of my own. I wasn't alone anymore. It wasn't in the way I had ever envisioned or thought I would want, but God knew much more than I what I really needed. My Prince Charming turned out to be my son, my little Prince, and God was the one on the white horse, my Knight in shining armor. God answered my prayer in such a different way than I thought He would. I have learned over and over again that His plans are much greater than my own.

"For I know the thoughts that I think toward you, says the Lord, thoughts of peace and not of evil, to give you a future and a hope. Then you will call upon Me and go and pray to Me, and I will listen to you. And you will seek Me and find Me, when you search for Me with all your heart."

- *Jeremiah 29:11-13*

PART THREE

♡

True Love's First Kiss

During my pregnancy, God gave me a clear vision and message of the purpose my son would have in this world when he was older and specific tasks to do for how to raise him according to his purpose. One thing I was told was to teach him to speak to all nations. That clear message with a purpose for my son's life and the specific ways to raise him freaked me out that I would fail horribly, yet it helped me to grow closer to God. No pressure, right?! God had given me commands for how to raise my son and how he was supposed to be when he got older when I wasn't even solid in my own relationship with God at that time. It was totally overwhelming, but knowing that God had a specific plan for my son and I was tasked with strict orders forced me to start taking God more seriously and not just casually. I didn't even like reading the Bible at first and I had to literally fight with myself inside convincing myself of the importance of it and the necessity. I knew my son would eventually emulate what he saw me doing and I refused to be a hypocrite. I had to practice what I was going to preach to him, otherwise we didn't stand a chance. I had no idea where to begin, so I just started cracking open the Bible and reading it out loud to my young son every night before bed. I started watching stuff about God on television. I knew about the Ten Commandments, but needed to know more about how to please God and be saved. I had a strong concern for my own salvation and especially my son's.

I had grown up "Christian," but had no idea how to actually be one or what it really meant. I started reading the Gospels; Matthew, Mark, Luke, then John, then I read 1 John as recommended by a preacher I had started listening to and liked. The more I read, the less jumbled and foriegn it became to me, and the more I began to understand. I had a thirst to learn more. I wasn't entirely convinced I wasn't delusional or having some sort of psychotic meltdown with my God Experiences, so I began to pursue God.

I assessed that in order to see whether or not God really was real or if I was just totally crazy, I would use the Scientific Method and do objective research on God. I wasn't really hoping God was real because I understood that if I became totally convinced that God was real, then my life would never be the same. I got that there was a weight of responsibility that came with God. I almost would have rather been totally crazy than for God to be real and all that came with it. I couldn't even have a good relationship with a guy at that time, so I was even less excited about the idea of a relationship with God, yet I continued to pursue the truth because I realized that my life and my son's depended on it. I had also always valued truth over comfort anyway. I figured that if God were real it would show on different levels. 1. It would be historical. There would be historical evidence to point to God's existence and biblical accuracy. 2. It would be tangible. I would have a personal experience with him that would be repeatable. God wouldn't just poof and talk to me one day then never show up again. And 3. It would be more than just me. Other people would be having experiences with God also. Keeping it brief, after about a year of pursuing the truth of God on those levels while reading my Bible I got enough evidence to convince me God was really real and I wasn't crazy. It was overwhelming, yet exciting. I had kept my newfound faith to myself in the early years until I was 100% convinced the God of the Holy Bible was real.

I began to read my Bible less out of curiosity and more out of devotion, seeking answers to my many questions, and also getting in the habit of incorporating it into my son's daily life. I started watching more televised sermons and devouring anything I could find that would help me in my new relationship with God. I was amazed with all that I found in the Bible that I had never even heard about. There was story after story of people who were similar to me. God came to the broken and transformed them, not because they were perfect or even deserving of it, but simply because He loved them and saw their heart beneath the brokenness. I read about the Prodigal Son and all the "wicked sinners." Then I read about the adulterous woman and the prostitute. My initial reaction was to turn my nose up at them and think degrading thoughts, but then I got a swift rebuke and realization that I was no different than them. All the times I had sex outside of marriage, I was committing the same sin as those women, I just wasn't getting paid for it like the prostitute. All those guys weren't my husband and I wasn't their wife. It didn't matter that I wasn't married at the time, nor were they. I was being adulterous to the future spouse that God had for me later on. I did not keep myself pure for him. I was no better than an adulteress or the prostitute. If God created each of us with a purpose and a role to fulfill, if He created our children the same and wove stories together, then surely He had a hand in who our spouses were supposed to be and it wasn't just by chance who we ended up with.

So grieved was I by the revelations that I was no better than the women I had turned my noses up, how deeply I had sinned against the only One that had truly loved me at that point, and that I'd even sinned and committed adultery against my future husband, I fell to my knees in anguish, praying for forgiveness, having just realized the true depth of my sins against an Almighty God. I prayed hard for forgiveness and that my sinful lifestyle would not cause my son to take the same path, but that God would protect my son from my sins. So grieved was I that after my crying out for forgiveness and vowing total repentance and completely offering up my life to God at that point, I was depressed for a good week by the weight of despair. How could I do such horrible things against a God who had sacrificed so much to save me? My sins caused those nails to be pounded into his flesh at his crucifixion. I was no better than anyone else, yet my love for Him increased the more I realized how even less deserving of His love, mercy, and grace I was. I committed myself to give my life back to the Lord, because it was the least I could do after He had done so much for me.

True love is a sacrifice.

Reading the Bible all the way through, I found so many accounts of how God healed, restored, redeemed, and saved people, all because of His unfailing Love. To realize that the God who created the Universe would humble Himself enough to not only save me multiple times in my present life, but did so close to 2,000 years before I was even born, was a truly life-changing moment. I couldn't even register not dedicating the rest of my life on earth to serving and honoring Him. No one in my life had loved me like that or been there for me in my darkest, lowest, ugliest moments and instead of condemning me, held me even tighter and loved me from the brokenness back into something real. It was true of the verse, "I loved because He first loved me." It began to be a delight to be obedient and keep the Commands, even though I still broke them many times in the early stages. I began to understand the practical reasons for the Laws and that, like my own earthly father had placed conditions to my staying with him for my own good, so God's Commands were meant as safeguards for us to keep us from hurting ourselves and others. It wasn't because He was a demanding tyrant, but because He so loves us He wants to protect us, just as evidenced by my earthly Dad.

True love sets boundaries.

I learned, unfathomably, that through sanctification my sins and shame could be washed clean. I left behind my old life of death and destruction to embrace a life with God that was full of hope. God had my back and has been with me through it all. A failed marriage and one last mistake of a relationship with a guy with demons taught me that if people fail us, leave us, abandon us, or hurt us, God never will. Hebrews 13:5 says, *"...I will not in any way fail you nor give you up nor leave you without support. I will not, I will not, I will not in any degree leave you helpless nor forsake you nor let you down..."*

True love lasts.

As a single and struggling mother living below the poverty level (less than $10,000 a year) and spending yet another Valentine's Day alone, single, and struggling through the days, this one particular song got stuck in my head as I was putting away laundry. It was *I Believe I Can Fly* by R. Kelly. I had not even heard that song in many years.

I was heavily feeling the bitter sting of divorce and yet another man leaving me. I didn't even want to count how many men had left me, and was wondering if any man would ever really love me or if I was going to be single for the rest of my life. Was I defective? Then that song annoyingly kept repeating in my head until I finally just started singing it out in my closet while I was putting away clothes, *"But now I know the meaning of True Love, I'm leaning on the Everlasting..."* Over and over until it finally clicked. The Everlasting One is God. By leaning on God and knowing Him, I can know and experience what true love is. True love is God. I didn't need a fleshly man to love me to make me feel I had worth or value. Nearly 2,000 years ago, a man was beaten, tortured, and nailed to a cross to die so I wouldn't have to. Before I ever needed saving, He sacrificed His life to save me. I already had the love of a devoted, dedicated man in my life, except this man was God incarnate in Jesus. This man was the Creator of the universe and all the good within it, and He still chose me. In my darkness, He pursued me. In my mess, He pulled me out of the pit and dusted me off. When I faltered and fell, he picked me up and helped me try again. When I couldn't love Him, He loved me anyway. There is no greater Love than that and no one more worthy and deserving of my lifelong dedication and devotion for.

True Love is God.

The more I followed God, the more things began to happen. I knew what True Love meant so I no longer sought fulfillment in a man, or any other human relationship for that matter. Knowing any relationship with a person would fall short of the love God had for me, I committed myself to no longer waste my time, energy, or heart with the roulette of casual dating. I vowed to be single and celibate, yes celibate, for the rest of my life or until God connected me with the man He intended to be my husband and one true earthly love, if He even had one for me. While so many others were pressuring me to date so I wouldn't be alone or to marry and get a father for my son (because it's just so easy apparently!) and while I was surrounded with warnings of the dangers of being a single mother and a boy not having a father figure in his life, I happily embraced my singleness and instead worked on my relationship with God, clinging tighter than ever to Him, secure in my relationship with God and my son.

True Love waits.

God taught me to value myself through being a mother. He taught me my body was a temple for Him to dwell in and a vessel for Him to use in this life. A Holy vessel should be treated with respect, so I started to act accordingly, purposing to begin taking care of myself, watching what I put into my body and how I treated it. He showed me my identity. I learned who I was in Christ. He is a King, and as His child that makes me a Princess, so I had better start owning it, not to be demanding or selfish, but to use the authority God gave me by being His child to make a dent in the darkness of this world and help heal the land. God showed me my ministry was for the broken. The people who feel unloved in this world like I did were those I am supposed to reach out to, share my story with, and show them the True Love that can only be found in God.

True Love adds value and worth.

As I began to get a foundation and learned how to walk on my own two feet, God began to really start healing my brokenness, bit by bit. I quickly learned that apart from God I could do nothing, not even heal myself, but with Him anything was possible. He had me throw away prescription meds I was taking to cope with the pain of divorce and to function through the day. I wasn't crazy, I didn't need them as a crutch, and I didn't need to poison my body and mind with those prescribed drugs. I let go of the crutch of prescriptions I'd been clinging to since I was thirteen and have never needed them since. God was greater than my "diagnoses."

True Love heals.

God gave me a platform. I began to share my story and minister to youth at the church I had started going to. I began sharing my testimony and connecting with teens who had felt no one understood them. Suddenly we connected through our brokenness and only a few short years after my own suicidal struggles, I was getting the overwhelming privilege to come along beside teens who were cutting, depressed, felt unheard and misunderstood, and struggled with suicidal thoughts. My negatives were turning out to be positives for others. I was able to help those and understand them the way I needed during my hardest times, but never had.

True Love redeems.

One Sunday after service, a member of my church family chased me down in the parking lot as I was about to get into my car. With tears in her eyes she told me that she had seen me walking and it was the first time she'd ever seen me hold my head up high and not have my head down to the ground with shoulders slumped. I hadn't realized my inner struggles were noticeable on the outside, but the perspective of someone else touched me deeply, especially as she wrapped me in a hug and was moved by my transformation. God had taken away the weight of my guilt and shame. He took away the sting of sin. He took away my belief that I wasn't worth anything good and had no value. Honestly, after a lifetime of negative voices and toxic environments, I am still struggling with many things and the enemy's voice that tells me lies, but slowly I am learning how to fight back and ignore the lies while embracing the truths. I am stronger than I ever was before and making progress on this healing journey. I am able, on most days, to walk with my head held high knowing I've been set free.

True Love restores.

I am thirty now and it has been over a decade since I first decided to follow God. It took a long time, with many more gut-wrenching heartbreaks, betrayals, tears, pain, fights, scars, battles, wilderness, and ugliness in-between. Through it all God was with me and I am finally out on the other side. I am no longer huddled up in that dark tunnel. I am standing out in freedom with my arms outstretched embracing the beauty and light in life, inhaling the fresh air and soaking in the warmth of all that life has to offer. God's love helped me to heal. It saved me. He gave me the precious love of a child. In November of 2014, He gave me the miraculous unconditional love of my best friend, the "One" man whom God had designed for me to get my Happily Ever After with, my true husband. A year and a half later God gave me another son. God grew me from one, to two, three, and four with many more family members added because of our marriage. The unconditional love of my husband, my children, God, and a growing community of people who have my back and cheer me on, are helping me to learn how to walk again, and I'm about to take off and soar. I am learning more and more about love by the people and experiences God connects me with. The Love of God is healing me, from my heart to my head. I can finally smile within my soul. I am not alone in the darkness anymore. I am a girl rescued by Love, not by a prince, but by a King.

Because of Him, I can know and give love. Because of Him, I am stronger than I've ever been before. Because of God, I am a *living* testimony of the power of True Love that can only come from Christ.

True love is SO worth it!

PART FOUR

The Real Meaning of Love

Growing up in an emotionally, verbally, and mentally abusive environment certainly made the definition of love confusing. In my heart, I knew what I grew up with was wrong. Love, real love, wasn't supposed to hurt like that. It was something I struggled with for many years, and only in this past year have I truly begun to see clearly what real love is and what it isn't, all because of developing my relationship with God. God is love, so only by and through Him can I learn what real love is supposed to be.

1 Corinthians 13 gives us a clear description of what love should and shouldn't be; *If I speak in the tongues of men or of angels, but do not have love, I am only a resounding gong or a clanging cymbal. If I have the gift of prophecy and can fathom all mysteries and all knowledge, and if I have a faith that can move mountains, but do not have love, I am nothing. If I give all I possess to the poor and give over my body to hardship that I may boast, but do not have love, I gain nothing. Love is patient, love is kind. It does not envy, it does not boast, it is not proud. It does not dishonor others, it is not self-seeking, it is not easily angered, it keeps no record of wrongs. Love does not delight in evil but rejoices with the truth. It always protects, always trusts, always hopes, always perseveres.*
Love never fails…. And now these three remain: faith, hope and love. But the greatest of these is love.

John 10:10 states, *The thief comes only to steal and kill and destroy; I have come that they may have life, and have it to the full.*

The more I grew in my relationship with God, the more clearly I saw the chasm between how certain members of my family treated me and how others did. All claimed to love me, yet one side of the chasm stole my joy, killed my spirit, and destroyed my value. The other side built up, encouraged, and edified. One side made me feel alone, worthless, like I'd be better off dead, and spoke death over me. The other side strengthened me, reminded me of my worth, and spoke life over me. A year ago from when I am writing this was when I was deep in a season of prayer and fasting. There were more brutal incidences between multiple family members on separate occasions that set me back. I realized from those incidents the reason why I had begun to regress in my progress. I was starting to get anxiety attacks again, feelings of depression and worthlessness, and began to withdraw. I had come so far and made so much progress, yet it seemed that just as I should be experiencing my total breakthrough, I was close to right back to where I had started from. I had a loving husband and two precious children. I had stability in all ways for the first time in my life. So why was I still stuck? Those incidents with my family members gave me a crystal-clear answer; my settings had changed, but my family remained the same with an open door to continue wounding me and speaking death over me. I was trying to mend the relationships in my own power, but they only served to harm me more. This time it was taking a toll on my own little family as well as the ministry God was setting me up for.

I became convicted that I needed to draw a line, again, yet this time a solid one for good. God impressed upon me the importance of setting up a strong barrier and to stop straddling the line. It was time for action. I spent a long season in prayer and fasting to ensure the precise way God wanted me to place the boundaries. Being solid in my relationship with God meant I no longer viewed my family as I had before. I deeply loved them. God had healed me from the nasty root of bitterness that had spread a poison within me. I wept for my family's poor choices. I wept for the family bond they could have had with me if only they'd stop hurting me in such cruel or selfish ways. My heart wanted to save them all. I had tried for so long to love them the way God had loved me, yet it only got worse. During that season of prayer and fasting, the Lord pressed in me that I had my own family to take care of. If I couldn't set the boundaries for my own self, then I needed to do it for my family. I couldn't be the wife and mother I needed to be when one nasty phone call from them left me in tears, or a passive-aggressive Facebook attack left me shaken and distraught, unable to focus on or enjoy my own family who truly loved me and actually needed me. My husband and children needed me whole. Those certain members of my extended family were keeping me broken. I realized that by continuing my relationship with those family members, I would never be fully healed. I would never get the breakthrough I needed, and I would never reach my full potential. Worse was that I would have to keep fighting the same battles as I had for three decades. Did I really want to endure this any longer? Instead of getting stronger, I was growing weaker. That was not healthy. That was not love. If they really loved me at all, they would want me whole and healthy. They were killing me, still. At nearly thirty, I was no longer a helpless kid stuck in a bad situation. This time, it was my own fault if I continued on in that toxic environment. It was time I finally stuck up for myself and did the one thing that was hardest for me to do. So great was my extended family's damage that I found it nearly impossible to truly love myself or treat myself right. One of the final things to click into place was my learning to love myself. I needed to step up and fight as hard for myself as I had and would for my family. Why could I easily protect them, but not myself? The hard truth was that I still was not fully convinced I was worth anything, but I chose to follow God.

In doing so, He set me free yet again. It has been almost a year since I have gone No Contact with my abusive, narcissist family members. It is painful. It was one of the hardest things

I've ever had to do, and that's saying a lot. It was not easy, nor fun, and I had no joy, but deep sadness from it. However, once the fear of their retaliation dissipated and I regained my trusting in the Lord's promises, I began to feel strengthened. I began to finally breathe for the first time in my life and feel true freedom. I have had almost a year of not holding my breath and fighting an anxiety attack every time they called, came to visit, or had any contact with them at all. No longer am I consumed with the stabs of their words or the truth of their back-stabbing that always found its way back to me. I'm learning what real love is and what real family is supposed to be. By the goodness of God, I can finally say that I am surrounded by it, but only because I was forced to cut out the toxic relationships. I miss one of them. I don't miss the others at all or what they bring with them. I find myself longing for my mother at times, aching almost, but then I remember it is only the image of what I wished she was that I crave. I remember how much it hurts being in a relationship with her, and each of the others. Having to divorce family is painful, but staying with them hurts far worse.

I have forgiven them, even long before I had to cut them and their poison out of my life. I am not consumed with thoughts of them. There is no bitterness or hate in me. I feel sorry for them and what they could have. Their version of forgiveness was that they could continue hurting me and each time I had to allow it without any consequences on their part. God showed me that's not what love or forgiveness is. Forgiveness means refusing to allow the hurt to cause me to sin or have it suck the joy and promise from my life. It means setting healthy boundaries for myself and my family. It does not mean having to allow them in my life at all, or to let them continue to abuse me. It has given me the ability to very carefully share my story by choosing to still honor them by not sharing every sordid detail of their lives, but only the most crucial to being able to relay the depth of my story. I could take this time when I have your attention to share all the worst stories, but God is greater than that, and that's not what love is either. God tells us in Luke chapter 6 to *"Love your enemies, do good to those who hate you, bless those who curse you, pray for those who mistreat you. If someone slaps you on one cheek, turn to them the other also. If someone takes your coat, do not withhold your shirt from them. Give to everyone who asks you, and if anyone takes what belongs to you, do not demand it back. Do to others as you would have them do to you.*

"If you love those who love you, what credit is that to you? Even sinners love those who love them. And if you do good to those who are good to you, what credit is that to you? Even sinners do that. And if you lend to those from whom you expect repayment, what credit is that to you? Even sinners lend to sinners, expecting to be repaid in full. But love your enemies, do good to them, and lend to them without expecting to get anything back. Then your reward will be great, and you will be children of the Most High, because he is kind to the ungrateful and wicked. Be merciful, just as your Father is merciful.

I can love them without having to let them into my life. Only the power of God can break such mighty chains and enable me to love those that curse me and continuously use and abuse me without letting them in to beat me down again. God allowed my circumstances, but He didn't intend for me to remain a slave there. He set me free to share my story with anyone who will listen.

Real love can hurt sometimes because it requires a sacrifice of us laying down our lives for someone else. The difference between real love and abusive love is that being a victim and sacrificing are not the same thing. A victim is beaten down, abused, made to believe they are worthless and dependent on the abuser. That kind of relationship is destructive. Real sacrificial love is beautiful, bears great fruit, heals, encourages, and strengthens. Abusive relationships tear down and destroy. A love sacrifice is foregoing something one wants because seeing the other person happy means more. There is no fear in real love, for *perfect love casts out fear*, as stated in 1 John 4:18.

Only in setting healthy boundaries around myself and my family am I finally able to see it all clearly and heal properly. I am finally learning to love myself, the hardest lesson of all, but I'm worth it. I can finally be the wife, mother, friend, and world changer that I was created to be. It is amazing how alive I feel and how much I love life now. Every day is a treasure. I marvel in much of God's Creations. Every person is a treasure. A fire burns in my heart to reach the lost and broken in this world, the people who think they are overlooked or forgotten. I long to share with everyone the true love that is only found in God, with a special place in my heart for the Undesirables.

The toxicity of my extended family's abusive behavior held me back from so much in my life. It was a weight around my ankles and a noose around my neck. God has set me free. Like the Israelites, I am no longer a slave to a false version of "love," but am wrapped in the warmth and beauty of true love. God's love, and the people He has placed in my life now, are all part of the healing process and loving me back into a whole person.

There is hope.

Ever so often, in the rare moments where there is a pause in the busyness of my life, I marvel in awe at how far God has brought me and how close I was to missing out on everything I'd ever only dreamed of. Had I succeeded in my suicide, I would have missed out on finally being free, being truly loved, finding my purpose, being happy, and so much more. If I had succeeded in my suicide, so many lives would have forever been altered. My husband would not know the true unconditional love of a wife that esteems him and seeks to build him up to his highest potential. My precious children wouldn't even exist and the lives that have already touched would not be so. The ministry's my husband and I are a part of would be missing our unique gifts. Then there are the individual people whom God has placed in my life to love on and minister to, whom also teach me many things. I can honestly, not conceitedly say, the world is better for me being in it. My husband and I are already impacting so many lives in the short time we have been together, and we are only just beginning.

I have a vendetta against the devil. He tried to kill me, but God is greater. He tried to stop me, so I'm going to push harder. He tried to silence me, so I'm going to speak louder. He tried to destroy me, so I'm going to dedicate my life to bringing hope, love, and healing to others. I finally realize the potential of my worth and that I can use what the enemy intended for evil, to do great good in this world. So can you!

No matter what, no matter where you are or what you've done, how old or young you are, or whether you are all alone or surrounded by people; Nothing you have done is too great for God to forgive. God created each and every one of us, uniquely designed, for a special purpose and *such a time as this.* You are the only you there is. You are loved. You have value and worth. You have the ability to change the world and we can all do that through real love.

Death is the only permanence in life. Everything in life is for but a season. Some seasons just happen to be very long. If I were asked, knowing what I know now, if I would go back and do it all over again to end up where I am today, I would say yes. I would go back through the nightmare just to have what I do now. I have a husband who loves me, kids who teach me new things and grow my heart every day, I have a hope and a future, I have possibilities and joy, real friends and family. I have something to offer the world. Suicide would have taken all that away. I am grateful I lived. It took nearly three decades of being lost in the darkness to finally be free in the light. It was all worth it to be where I am now. God is so good!

SOME SCRIPTURES

Esther 4:14 – For if you remain silent at this time, relief and deliverance for the Jews will arise from another place, but you and your father's family will perish. And who knows but that you have come to your royal position for such a time as this?

1 Corinthians 16:14 – Do everything in love.

1 John 4:16 – And so we know and rely on the love God has for us. God is love. Whoever lives in love lives in God, and God in them.

Ephesians 4:2 – And so we know and rely on the love God has for us. God is love. Whoever lives in love lives in God, and God in them.

1 John 4:19 - We love because He first loved us.

Romans 12:9 - Love must be sincere. Hate what is evil; cling to what is good.

Isaiah 49:15-16 - Can a mother forget the baby at her breast and have no compassion on the child she has borne? Though she may forget, I will not forget you!
See, I have engraved you on the palms of my hands;

your walls are ever before me.

John 15:12 - My command is this: Love each other as I have loved you.

Romans 12:10 - Be devoted to one another in love. Honor one another above yourselves.

1 John 4:20 - Whoever claims to love God yet hates a brother or sister is a liar. For whoever does not love their brother and sister, whom they have seen, cannot love God, whom they have not seen.

1 Corinthians 2:9 - What no eye has seen, what no ear has heard, and what no human mind has conceived — the things God has prepared for those who love him.

1 Thessalonians 3:12 - May the Lord make your love increase and overflow for each other and for everyone else, just as ours does for you.

Romans 8:38-39 - For I am convinced that neither death nor life, neither angels nor demons, neither the present nor the future, nor any powers, neither height nor depth, nor anything else in all creation, will be able to separate us from the love of God that is in Christ Jesus our Lord.

1 John 4:8 - Whoever does not love does not know God, because God is love.

Mark 12:30 - Love the Lord your God with all your heart and with all your soul and with all your mind and with all your strength.

1 Corinthians 10:24 - No one should seek their own good, but the good of others.

2 Timothy 1:7 - For the Spirit God gave us does not make us timid, but gives us power, love and self-discipline.

John 3:16-21 - For God so loved the world that he gave his one and only Son, that whoever believes in him shall not perish but have eternal life. For God did not send his Son into the world to condemn the world, but to save the world through him. Whoever believes in him is not condemned, but whoever does not believe stands condemned already because they have not believed in the name of God's one and only Son. This is the verdict: Light has come into the world, but people loved darkness instead of light because their deeds were evil. Everyone who does evil hates the light, and will not come into the light for fear that their deeds will be exposed. But whoever lives by the truth comes into the light, so that it may be seen plainly that what they have done has been done in the sight of God.

ABOUT THE AUTHOR

Crystal A. Clemons is a Southwest Florida native that thrives on God, family, ministry, changing the world, and having as many adventures as possible. Among many other passions, she enjoys geocaching with her guys, science, toxin-free living and natural healing, as well as helping others see their potential and chase after their God-given dreams. She has a passion for homeschooling, natural living, education, and spreading as much light and love in the lives of those around her as possible.

Connect with her at crystalaclemons@yahoo.com.
She is also on Goodreads.com.

www.ingramcontent.com/pod-product-compliance
Lightning Source LLC
Chambersburg PA
CBHW021221020426
42331CB00003B/419